JACQUES HENRI LARTIGUE
PHOTOGRAPHER

JACQUES HENRI LARTIGUE

PHOTOGRAPHER

Vicki Goldberg

Thames and Hudson

On June 29, 1979, the photographs of Jacques Henri Lartigue were donated to the French state,
which assigned the conservation, administration, and circulation of this collection to the Association des Amis
de Jacques Henri Lartigue under the auspices of the Mission du Patrimoine Photographique
within the Ministry of Culture and Communication.

First published in Great Britain in 1998 by
Thames and Hudson Ltd, London

Copyright © 1998 Editions Nathan, Paris
Photographs copyright © 1998 Ministère de la Culture
et de la Communication, France

British Library Cataloguing-in-Publication Data
A catalogue record for this book is available from the British Library

ISBN 0-500-54226-0

Printed in Switzerland

All happiness is a kind of innocence.

Marguerite Yourcenar

Lartigue: The Passions of a Child and the Eye of an Adult

Jacques Henri Lartigue thought that perhaps it was God who gave him his first camera. Or at least someone who might have been mistaken for him. "*Papa*," he wrote in a journal he reconstructed from childhood memories, "*il ressemble au Bon Dieu (c'est peut-être même bien lui, déguisé?), il vient de me dire: 'Je vais te donner un vrai appareil de photographie!*'" [As for Daddy, he is like God (and may even be him, in disguise), and has just told me: "I'm going to give you a real camera!"] His father took photographs himself and taught the boy how to develop them. This was late in 1901, when Jacques Lartigue was seven years old.[1]

A religious boy who became a religious man, he wrote in the same journal, apparently in total seriousness, that by the age of thirteen he knew that God had guaranteed his happiness: "*J'aime le Bon Dieu et je sais que je serai toujours heureux grâce à Lui.*"[2] [I love God and I know I will always be happy, thanks to Him.] And all his life, from earliest boyhood on, he devoted a kind of religious fervor to preserving the happiness which God had granted him so young, consecrating to that service the camera given him by God's surrogate.

The world through Lartigue's camera was composed of antics and inventions, fashion and coquetry, sun, wind, languor, and dreams – a place where cars were handsome and parasols gracious, where people at leisure sported white trousers on the beach. No one cried there, for every desire was sated with delirious speed, in an amusing suspension of gravity, and in an abundance of feminine beauty. Almost the only reminder of ordinary sorrow was the vast and relentless loneliness of the sea.

Lartigue considered happiness both a grace and a goal. He elected himself conservator of the contentment he recognized as his birthright. When little, he invented what he called an "eye-trap"; by staring widely and then blinking he managed to print a scene in all its liveliness on his brain. A few days after this great discovery, he woke up to find the technique no longer worked and immediately fell sick. When he recovered, he resolved to reconstruct this wonderful effect by other means.

He became the caretaker of his own felicity, with three means of preserving it: photography, painting (or drawing), and writing. When the parent who so resembled *le Bon Dieu* gave him his first camera, he determined to photograph everything, *everything*, so he would no longer have to regret forsaking the joys of a country house for Paris, but could take them with him tucked into his photographs.[3]

His most fervent wish was to remain a child. By the time he was six, according to his journals, he was dismayed at the prospect of growing up and getting bigger.[4] It is not so uncommon for children, especially if they are cosseted and spoiled, to be reluctant to grow up. Jacques, born five years later than his brother, Zissou, seems to have shared with his mother a fantasy that he would always be her little baby.[5]

He was fortunate in many ways. He was born at the right place, at the right time, to the right family. The Lartigues had money and ingenuity – several of the men in the family were inventors and engineers – plus warmth and a sense of adventure. They scarcely bothered with his education but imbued him with a strong attachment to culture. The talents the boy was born with were encouraged, and the weaknesses he developed contributed in a peculiar way to his original enterprise.

When he did grow up he was evidently entirely charming – and also self-centered, emotionally detached (though often enough in love), a spectator who cursed his own inability to be involved, and so intent on a life of bliss that he excised earthly problems from his memory bank whenever possible.[6] In his paintings, photographs, and writings he ignored as best he could the hellish side of the era in which he lived. All of which contributed to a body of work that is, as he meant it to be, delightful, amusing, and at moments simply astonishing.

The right place and time: Part of the enchantment of Lartigue's early photographs lies in the sparkle of a long-gone era and the nostalgia that clings to it. He viewed the end of the *belle époque* from a singular domestic vantage point, with a gleeful emphasis on the technological changes in transport and speed, and with the preternaturally alert eye of an eager, curious, perceptive boy. His eccentric family in itself fairly guaranteed that his pictures would be uncommon. His brother, like his grandfather and great-uncle, had a knack, indeed a mania, for inventions – makeshift cars, boats concocted from tires, homemade airplanes. Relatives and playmates ran at these pell-mell, racing and jousting, jumping, tumbling, crashing. Jacques, himself too small, was kept from joining in by the bigger boys and became a spectator for life.

In early 1902, with a camera too big for a little boy and exposures excruciatingly long, he took a few rather standard, posed family portraits. That same year, when he turned eight, his father gave him a Spido-Gaumont stereoscopic camera,[7] and he soon learned to use it to stop action. Stereo cameras had succeeded in stopping slow movements, like men and women walking in the streets, as early as the 1850s, and by the end of the century, fast shutter speeds and emulsions had captured the horse at full gallop and made the snapshot a reality.

Lartigue, who never wanted to let the moment go, was especially entranced by moments that could not last. His cat cooperated by jumping, and Lartigue coaxed whoever was not already racing downhill, or defying gravity, to try out the air: tossing balls, sailing down stairs, jumping off walls. He turned their transitory shapes into lasting emblems: the spread-eagled cat, the perilous angle of legs leaving the ground with a runaway glider, the exploded zigzag of a woman in a long dress running down the beach with her veil and coat following in the wind. He relished the magical fleeting instant when photography puts the laws of gravity on hold.

The right family at the right time: His father, who bought an electric automobile in 1902 and faster cars in the following years, avidly followed automobile races and early attempts to fly. In modern history there has probably never been a little boy who was not fascinated by cars and planes, but Jacques Lartigue came into the world just as technology began laughing at space and time.

At the Universal Exposition in Paris in 1900, what struck the young Lartigue as the largest hall was the Galerie des Machines.[8] He noted: "*Ces choses compliquées ne m'intéressent pas du tout.*"[9] [Those complicated things don't interest me at all.] It bulked so large in deference to a revolution that was still in process. That year a French Panhard won the first international championship automobile race, averaging 62 kilometers per hour on the road from Paris to Lyons. The same year Kodak introduced the Brownie, the box camera so small that even children less dedicated than Lartigue could make pictures. A mere three years later, Wilbur Wright would fly a motorized, heavier-than-air plane for fifty-nine seconds over the dunes of Kitty Hawk, North Carolina.

The world was in perpetual motion. Lartigue ran after every attempt, however whimsical or triumphant, to go faster, farther, higher on wheels or on wings. In 1912, when he photographed *Delage Automobile, A.C.F. Grand Prix* (Automobile Club de France), everything moved: a narrow slit in his focal-plane shutter traveled rapidly across the plate like a curtain, registering some parts of the scene a tiny fraction of a second later than others. Spectators seemed to tilt, and the wheel of the car elastically changed shape. Photographing another racing car that day, Lartigue initiated a new method, which consisted of keeping his camera still while moving himself: "*Je la photographie (180 à l'heure) en pivotant un peu sur moi même pour la conserver dans mon viseur. C'est la première fois que je fais ça!*"[10] [I photographed it (doing 180 kilometers per hour) turning a little as I did so, to keep it in my viewfinder. It was the first time I did that!]

The earth rushed by and the once-familiar, everyday sky was invaded by fragile machines; enthusiastically, the boy recorded the shift. A couple took their baby out for an unexceptional airing in a stroller, but the very air had changed: a plane hovering low to the ground interrupted the scene, while high in the empty space above, another one stained the sky.

Lartigue had an exquisite appreciation of the bizarre and complex shapes of his era: the extravagant confections and flightless wings women wore on their heads, the extraterrestrial architecture of great kites, the gliders and planes like fanciful and delicate cages intended to trap air.

But he also understood, or was lucky enough to register and smart enough not to delete, the odd outlines people assume as they walk, outlines the eye does not fully notice because it does not see isolated moments, stopped in time. He could trace the more complicated silhouettes that overlapping figures produce as well, and the even more surprising and marvelous incorporeal shapes that fill the spaces between people and things.

And then his camera would note down figures or boats or trees that unexpectedly intruded on the scene and made witty comments on foreground shapes by echoing, inverting, subverting, or completing them. In short, Lartigue commanded a specifically photographic vision of the world that already had precedents, but had neither been explicitly worked out nor appreciated as a style.

The style entailed putting a high value on the momentary, the unstable, and the unbalanced; Lartigue's childish glee and the new century's inventions pushed this to a new level. In the ordinary life lived outside of cars and airplanes, momentariness generally meant casual, unconscious, and unobserved (or at least uncelebrated) movements or expressions or relationships – the not-so-negligible events that occur between poses struck for public display.

The Realist painters in the third quarter of the nineteenth century had begun to record this kind of momentary event on canvas as part of their radical attempt to depict contemporary life in all its irregular and haphazard forms. Manet had a feeling for it; Degas expressed it vividly. Photography probably influenced both these painters – Degas took photographs himself – and the qualities they sought to achieve in their art came naturally to a mechanical medium.

When photographers had stumbled on such things as a previously unperceived stage in the human gait or an awkward overlap as people crossed paths, the resulting images had been recognized as scientific discoveries or photographic mistakes, but not as anything of artistic value. Indeed, the kinds of spiky hybrids made by adjacent parasols, the abrupt cropping of faces or figures seen too close, the elaborately outlined spaces between people, did not even begin to achieve full artistic status until the 35mm camera came along.

But the style was already germinating in Lartigue's infancy, principally in some early street photography and, more by mistake than otherwise, in the growing accumulation of amateur snapshots, for the camera in its voraciousness makes such decisions without any encouragement from the operator.

When he started taking photographs, Lartigue was probably too young to be aware of artistic images, aside from his father's photographs and possibly illustrated books, yet he articulated a style that was only being whispered at that time.

A product of his family and of his times, he recorded the playful, thrilling, suspenseful, and absurd aspects of both with rare ardor and discrimination. He was uncommonly focused in every way, and his eye was simply better than anyone had a right to expect at his age. History provided him with a cornucopia of inventions, including a camera with a fast lens, and he responded with the passions of a child and the eye of an adult.

He was in fact a photographic anomaly: a child prodigy. Although children are increasingly taught photography in schools and many produce good pictures, it is hard to think of another example in the history of the medium of someone Lartigue's age who consistently took remarkable photographs. The child was certainly lucky in his subject matter, but luck is not gracious enough to sustain such a body of work. Some part of its appeal may be the reflection of a little boy's spirit, more rambunctious than his body, as he grew up protected in a world fairly bursting with exciting games and discoveries. But photography generally depends on perceptions, discriminations, and subtle judgments not usually thought available to one so young.

He was particularly alive in all his senses, highly tuned to sounds and smells as well as sight – "*Seulement, moi, ce ne sont pas des pensées que je voudrais attraper au piège mais l'odeur de mon bonheur!*"[11] [Except that what I would like to capture aren't thoughts, but the scent of my happiness!] Small, not strong, and sickly, he had a lot of time to cultivate his senses, practice his talent for drawing, burnish his avid powers of observation.

He turned his eye on women and female decor early. His journal says he began drawing pictures of women wearing hats and rings at the age of eight[12] and by fourteen was "*étourdi de plaisir*" [dizzy with pleasure] at the mere thought of taking his camera into the Bois de Boulogne to find "*Elle.*" "*Elle*" was "*la dame très attifée, très à la mode, très ridicule… ou très jolie*" [the very made-up, very fashionable, very ridiculous… or very pretty lady] whose picture he would snap despite the occasional wrath of a gentleman by her side.[13]

Here was another spectacle for his hungry camera to feast on. The women who paraded past his lens were dazzling, self-created displays, as carefully groomed and often as exotic as tropical birds. Lartigue noticed that some wore lip rouge as if they were on stage, a sign of changing ideas of feminine appeal. If the men felt called upon to defend them against photography, that was another sign of the times: ever since the 1880s, when hand cameras made outdoor photography easier, women (and some men) had felt attacked by the legions of amateurs on the prowl for pictures.[14]

Lartigue caught all the nuances of high-heeled gait and swishing skirts: hats as big as architecture, pleated fichus, fringes, finicky dogs, womanly figures tailored to within an inch of flirtation. At least twice he snapped the appreciative and speculative glances that men who thought themselves unobserved cast at items on display.

He relished the clothes as much as the women, and their strategies for making women beautiful. A case could be made for calling Lartigue the first fashion photographer (*Vogue* did not hire Baron de Meyer, its first staff photographer, until 1914), though he neither recognized this role nor published the pictures. When Lartigue's previously unknown photographs were finally discovered in the 1960s, Cecil Beaton drew on *Carriage Day at the Races at Auteuil, Paris, 23 June 1911,* that rhapsody of hips and stripes, for his costume designs for *My Fair Lady*.[15] (Lartigue had essentially been a painter of some repute in France until his early photographic work was discovered, almost by chance, by John Szarkowski, who then put on an exhibition of his photographs at the Museum of Modern Art in New York in 1963.)

Once World War I began, Lartigue withdrew for most of his long life from the history of his times.[16] Too underweight to serve in the military, he was assigned to chauffeur officers around Paris. He seldom photographed the effects of war and the ugly episodes he saw. His journals retreated from the evidence, barely noting: "The war goes on. Friends die. Good weather. My first mistress (the most desirable woman in Paris). Good weather."

He explained to these private pages that his retreat was fully conscious. His reconstructed journal of 1907 had attributed his happiness to the habit of effacing bad memories and embellishing the good.[17] Now he wrote, "*La guerre, si ce 'journal' n'en parle pas, c'est d'abord que ce n'est pas un 'journal.' C'est mon petit jeu secret pour essayer de conserver des joies ou mon bonheur, mon immense bonheur tout parfumé de choses qu'on n'explique pas. Et en même temps c'est une protection. Une protection contre 'l'excès de bonheur.'*"[18] [If this "journal" doesn't mention the war, it is first of all because this is *not* a "journal." It is my little secret ruse for preserving joys or my happiness, my immense happiness, all perfumed with inexplicable things. And at the same time it's protection. Protection against "too much happiness."] While the world burned he tended his silken memories, thus avoiding the pit of lethargy, or perhaps the loss of control.

In 1919 he married Bibi Messager, daughter of the composer André Messager, and embarked on the life of a millionaire without much money, painting Bibi and flowers, gliding about the Riviera, Paris, and London, going to the theater every night to see his close friends Sacha Guitry and Yvonne Printemps perform, photographing Bibi, the races, sunlight, and the sea, a perfumed life. It was still possible to make an art of living then, and he did.

Though Europe had lost its innocence somewhere in among the trenches, and disillusion had seeped into daily life, Lartigue by now was intent on chronicling his own existence rather than anyone else's. Car and bicycle races still intrigued him, technological advance did not. He had a son, and a daughter who died in infancy. Bibi left him for another man, other women came along, and a Depression, and fascism. He had a brief second marriage and a lasting third one. Steadfastly, he kept his eye on the garden of earthly delights.

The eye that had been so quick to grasp the possibilities of photographic composition when he was still a child had become increasingly sophisticated. The twin lenses of his Klapp Nettel stereoscopic camera, which took two 6 x 6 cm photographs, could be converted to a single-lens format taking one 6 x 13 cm picture. Lartigue exploited this elongated frame with a balancing act of precarious juxtapositions, disjunct scales, and mysterious figures hovering in the wings.

He held his camera less than a meter away from a racing car, disrupting the scale so thoroughly that a spectator on the far side might have strayed in from another space. A small figure of a man running in front of an incoming wave is overshadowed by a monstrously large fellow, who bears no connection to him, in the foreground. The lively relations between figures in Lartigue's early pictures began to break down, and normative space now and then threatened to slip its moorings.

A faint tinge of melancholy lingers in some images: his beloved Bibi dwarfed by objects that expand as she seems to shrink; her figure, isolated and small, in indifferent cities, or standing on a terrace with his mother before the sea.

Lartigue was increasingly troubled by his own detachment from life. "*Mon égoisme m'effare. Il y a en moi un spectateur qui regarde sans se soucier d'aucune contingence, sans savoir si ce qui se passe est sérieux, triste, important, drôle ou non. Une espèce d'habitant d'étoile venu sur terre uniquement pour jouir du spectacle. Un spectateur pour qui tout est marionette, même – et surtout – moi!*"[19] [My self-centeredness alarms me. There is a spectator in me who watches, with no concern for specific events, without knowing if what is happening is serious, sad, important, funny, or not. A breed of extraterrestrial, who has come to Earth simply to enjoy the show. A spectator for whom everything is puppetry, even – and especially – me!]

Several images, one taken in the first decade of the century, focus on a lone man seen from behind, as if he could be any one of us, watching the sea beat powerfully against rocks or walls. This is a Romantic theme, man confronting the indomitable force of nature, an image repeatedly explored in paintings like Caspar David Friedrich's 1809 *Monk by the Sea*.

When he was very small, Jacques Lartigue worried that this was precisely the cost of growing up: "*Découvrir tout à coup l'impuissance vertigineuse d'être un petit humain aux prises avec la vérité des choses, est-ce cela 'grandir'?*"[20] [To discover suddenly the staggering helplessness of being a little human being coming to grips with the truth of things, is that "growing up"?] He remained a spectator all his life, and we are the beneficiaries. He tried to remain a boy and his spirit succeeded, but time could not be stopped – except, of course, in photographs.

Vicki Goldberg

1. Jacques Henri Lartigue, *Mémoires sans mémoire* (Paris: Editions Robert Laffont, 1975), p. 34. He did not begin keeping a regular journal until 1911.
2. *Mémoires* for 1907, p. 66.
3. *Mémoires* for 1901, p. 35.
4. *Mémoires* for 1900, p. 24.
5. *Mémoires* for 1905, p. 58.
6. See Shelley Rice, "Lartigue, L'Empailleur de Bonheur," in *Jacques Henri Lartigue: Le choix du bonheur* (Paris: Editions La Manufacture, 1992), p. 262, for information on how he rewrote his memoirs. This essay astutely assays Lartigue's character and his lifetime project. Michel Frizot, "L'ombre et le reflect," in *Le passé composé* (Paris: Centre National de la Photographie et L'Association des Amis de Jacques Henri Lartigue, 1984), discusses the way Lartigue cropped his 6 x 13 photographs in the 1920s when making up his photo albums.
7. Florette Lartigue, *Jacques Henri Lartigue: La traversée du siècle* (Paris: Bordas, 1990), p. 24.
8. *Mémoires* for 1900, p. 26.
9. *Mémoires* for 1900, p. 26.
10. *Mémoires* for 1912, p. 127.
11. Jacques Henri Lartigue, *L'Emerveillé: écrit à mesure 1923–31* (Stock, 1981), p. 273.
12. *Mémoires* for 1902, p. 44.
13. *Mémoires* for 1910, pp. 80–81.
14. See Heinz K. Henisch and Bridget A. Henisch, *The Photographic Experience, 1839–1914: Images and Attitudes* (University Park, Pennsylvania: The Pennsylvania State University Press, 1993), p. 263; and Vicki Goldberg, *The Power of Photography: How Photographs Changed Our Lives* (New York: Abbeville Press, 1991), pp. 113–115.
15. Florette Lartigue, *Lartigue: La traversée*, p. 40.
16. Rice, "L'Empailleur," p. 27, says that the year 1914 gave a double impetus to Lartigue's withdrawal into himself: his father was shot three times, not fatally, by a deranged man, and the younger Lartigue was rejected for service at the front. In neither case was he where the action was.
17. *Mémoires* for 1907, p. 72.
18. *Mémoires* for 1917, p. 273.
19. *L'Emerveillé*, p. 220.
20. *Mémoires* for 1900, p. 33.

*All happiness is a masterpiece: the slightest
mistake throws it off, the slightest hesitation
corrupts it, the slightest heaviness mars it,
the slightest foolishness makes it dull.*

MARGUERITE YOURCENAR

2

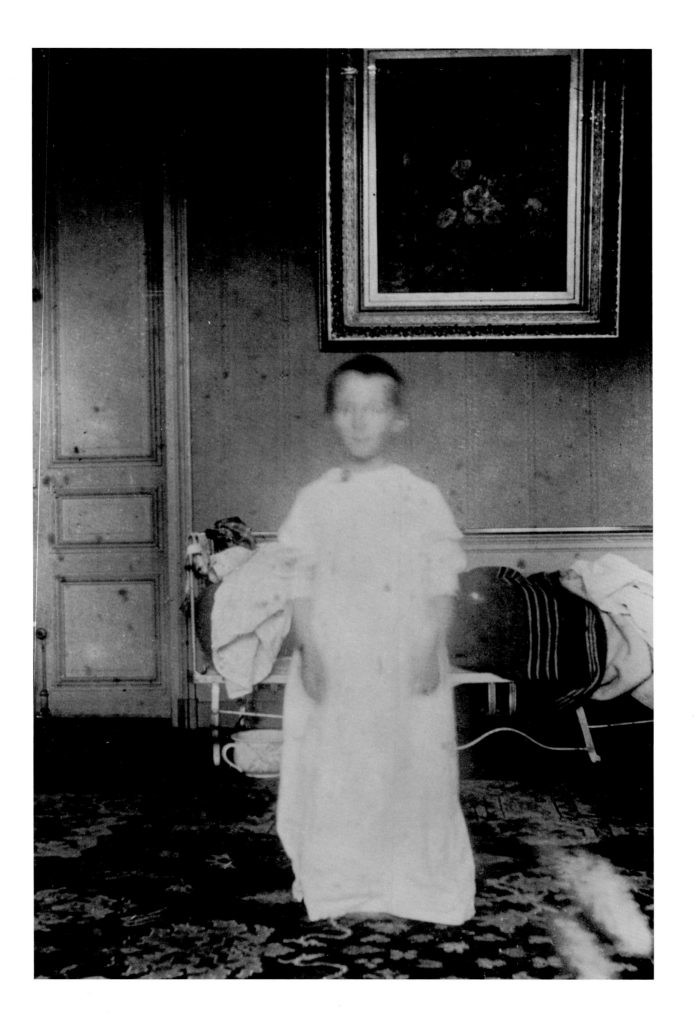

We must create a happiness that can follow us in every age.

Montesquieu

Captions written by Jacques Henri Lartigue

1 My nanny Dudu, Paris, 1904.

2 My garden, Pont-de-l'Arche, 1904.

3 My cat Zizi, Paris, 1904.

4 Mardi Gras with Bouboutte, Louis, Robert, and Zissou, Paris, 1903.

5 Bouboutte, Rouzat, 1908.

6 Aunt Yéyé, my little cousin Dédé, Uncle Auguste, Daddy, Zissou, Mummy, and Marcelle, Pont-de-l'Arche, 1902. First photo taken absolutely by myself with my 13 x 18 cm plate camera.

7 My uncle Auguste and my cousin Dédé in my room, Paris, 1906.

8 Rico Broadwater and James, the valet, Rouzat, 1910.

9 Daddy and Mummy, Pont-de-l'Arche, 1902 (my second photo).

10 My uncle Auguste, my cousin Dédé, and my cousin Marcelle, Pont-de-l'Arche, 1903.

11 My cousin Bichonnade, Paris, 1905.

12 My cousin André Haguet, known as Dédé, Paris, 1906.

13 Zissou dressed as a ghost, Villa "Les Marronniers," Châtelguyon, July 1905.

14 Zissou and Madeleine Thibault, Rouzat, 1911.

15 A kite outing, Rouzat, 1911.

16 Portrait of Louis, July 1904.

17 My cousin Simone in the park at Saint-Cloud, 1913.

18 Skating on the lake in the Bois de Boulogne, Paris, December 1906.

19 Raymond Van Weers, known as Oléo, Rouzat, 1908.

20 Monsieur Folletête and Tupy, Paris, March 1912.

21 Le Havre, 1909.

22 Paris–Tours motorcycle race, a contestant passing through Orléans, 1912.

23 Paris–Tours motorcycle race, a contestant passing through Orléans, 1912.

24 Grandmother, Mummy, and I with my first camera, Bois de Boulogne, Paris, 1903.

25 Avenue du Bois de Boulogne, Paris, January 1911.

26 In front of the Chinese Pavilion, Porte Dauphine, Paris, April 1911.

27 In front of the Dauphine Pavilion, at the Club de l'Etrier, Paris, 1912.

28 Avenue du Bois de Boulogne, Paris, January 1911.

29 Avenue du Bois de Boulogne, Paris, May 1911.

30 Avenue des Acacias, Paris, 1911.

31 Avenue des Acacias, Paris, 1911.

32 At the races at Auteuil, 1911.

33 Carriage Day at the races at Auteuil, Paris, 1911.

34 Carriage Day at the races at Auteuil, Paris, 1911.

35 At the races at Auteuil, 1912.

36 The Duke of Montpensier's wedding, Rendan, August 1921.

37 Marcelle's First Communion, Le Mans, 1907.

38 Marthe Chenal at the Racing Club de France, Paris, May 1916.

39 Charity Day for the wounded, Vichy, 1915.

40 Janine Dupuis in her father's Pic-Pic, La Baule, 1915.

41 Nice, April 17, 1912.

42 At the Carlton, Vichy, August 1922.

43 The end of the slide, Luna Park, Paris, June 1909.

44 Gaby Deslys during the filming of *Bouclette*, Casino de Paris, February 1918.

45 Bibi, 1923.

46 Bibi, I, and Granny, back in Paris, April 1920.

47 Mummy, Daddy, Yves, the chauffeur, and Monsieur Laroze on a car trip, October 1911.

48 Tony Lekain, Bibi, and Suzy Vernon, Royan, September 1926.

49 Guitty (Marguerite Bourcart) in Biarritz, 1905.

50 My cousin Simone, Villerville, 1904.

51 Kite in Biarritz, 1905.

52 Zissou and the ZYX 21, Rouzat, 1908.

53 The ZYX 24 takes off... Piroux, Zissou, Georges, Louis, Dédé, and Robert try to take off with it, Rouzat, September 1910.

54 The crowd gathered for Gabriel Voisin's first public flight in the glider *Archdeacon*, Merlimont, April 1904.

55 Zissou with Gabriel Voisin's aeroplane, Merlimont, April 1904.

56 Zissou at the bar of the Adour River, Biarritz, February 1909.

57 Madeleine and Marthe Van Weers, known as Bichonnade and Bouboutte, Dieppe, 1908.

58 Storm in Dieppe, December 1928.

59 Marthe Chenal, Villers, August 1916.

60 Biarritz, September 1917.

61 The dirigible *Ville de Paris*, Sartrouville, 1907.

62 Deauville, 1919.

63 Testing a scale model at the Trocadero, Paris, February 1908.

64 Second light-aircraft competition at the cycling track of the Parc des Princes, Paris, November 24, 1912.

65 The aeroplane *Antoinette*, Issy-les-Moulineaux, October 1910.

66 Maurice Farman in a biplane, Buc, November 1911.

67 *Frégate*, Issy-les-Moulineaux, October 1909.

68 Zissou in Amérigo's slipstream, Buc, November 1911.

69 Audemars in a Blériot aeroplane, Vichy, September 1912.

70 Mathieu in a Farman, Issy-les-Moulineaux, January 1911.

71 The Gaillon road, 1912.

72 The great racer Nazzaro signals to Wagner to accelerate. A.C.F. [Automobile Club de France] Grand Prix, Dieppe circuit, June 26, 1912.

73 Jenatzy's famous Mercedes, Gordon-Bennett Cup, Auvergne circuit, July 1905.

74 My "great hero" Duray, in a Lorraine-Dietrich, Auvergne circuit, 1905.

75 Start of the Antibes Grand Prix, May 1929.

76 Start of the A.C.F. Grand Prix, Sarthe circuit, 1906.

77 Delage automobile, A.C.F. Grand Prix, Dieppe circuit, June 26, 1912.

78 A.C.F. Grand Prix, Lyons circuit, 1914.

79 San Sebastián Grand Prix, July 1927.

80 Montlhéry racetrack, 1924.

81 Antibes Grand Prix, May 1929.

82 Grand Prix Automobile, La Baule, August 1929.

Chronology

1894. June 13: Jacques Henri Lartigue is born in Courbevoie, in his parents' home. He is their second son after Maurice, nicknamed Zissou, who was born August 2, 1889.

1899. The Lartigue family leaves Courbevoie to go and live on the boulevard Emile-Augier in Paris.

1900. With his father's help, Jacques Lartigue takes his first photographs. He begins to jot down on pieces of paper his first impressions and reflections, which will gradually become his journal.

1901. The Lartigue family moves to a town house at 40 rue Cortambert in Paris. Henri Lartigue also purchases a property in Pont-de-l'Arche, Eure.

1902. Henri Lartigue gives Jacques his first camera and, during his summer vacation in Pont-de-l'Arche, the child takes and develops his first photographs on his own. He begins to paste them and lay them out in notebooks.

1903. For fun, he uses sunlight to darken printing-out paper around various objects, which makes them appear as ephemeral white silhouettes.

1904. He discovers the possibility of superimposing images and makes photographs of "ghosts."
April 3: On the beach at Merlimont, he photographs Gabriel Voisin taking off in the glider *Archdeacon*.

1905. Henri Lartigue buys the Château de Rouzat in the Puy-de-Dôme and has it restored.

1906. Henri Lartigue buys his first automobile, a Panhard Levassor. Maurice begins to build flying machines in the former fermentation room of the Château de Rouzat. At the Automobile Club de France Grand Prix, on the Sarthe circuit, Jacques meets the photographer Simons from the newspaper *La Vie au grand air*.

1907. May 2: Jacques Lartigue makes his First Communion. In October, he begins to spend time regularly at the airfield at Issy-les-Moulineaux. The Lumière brothers perfect the autochrome process.

1908. Thanks to being a member of the Ligue Aérienne [Aerial League], to which every pilot belongs, Jacques Lartigue is able to photograph Roland Garros, Latham, Paulhan, Lefèvre, Farman, Blériot...

1910. In the course of his strolls in the Bois de Boulogne, Jacques Lartigue begins to photograph fashionable women.

1911. January: Exasperated by those who claim the weather is always bad, Jacques Lartigue makes a daily note of the weather in a small notebook. At the Sorbonne, he takes a course under Marius Aubert, assistant to Gabriel Lippmann, who has perfected a color photographic process.
February: The Lartigue family moves to a town house at 15 rue Leroux, in the 16th arrondissement in Paris, where they will remain.
For the first time, Jacques Lartigue sells his photographs, to the newspaper *La Vie au grand air*. His father's chauffeur, Yves, teaches him to drive. He makes his first movie, in the Bois de Boulogne, with a camera given him by his father.

1913. January: He photographs Santos-Dumont, Graham White, and Max Linder in Saint Moritz.

1914. January: He films and photographs Lesseps aboard his propeller-sleigh. He sells his sports films to Actualités Pathé.
March 17: Jacques Lartigue is deferred on medical grounds by the review board.
August 3: Germany declares war on France.

1915. June: Jacques Lartigue wants to become a painter, and so takes a few courses at the Académie Jullian.

1916. Because he now can drive fast and well, he offers his and his race car's services to doctors in Paris hospitals caring for those wounded in the war.
November 1: His friend Jean Dary, the aviator, takes him for his first flight in a "crate."

1917. May 19: He meets Madeleine Messager, whom he will nickname Bibi.

1918. June 5: Jacques Lartigue announces that he has done his first oil painting.
November 11: The armistice is signed.
An epidemic of Spanish influenza strikes many people the Lartigue family knows.

1919. December 17: Jacques Lartigue marries Madeleine Messager, daughter of the composer André Messager, who had been director of the Comic Opera at Covent Garden, London, then of the Paris Opéra.

1921. January 6: Birth of Florette Orméa, who will become Florette Lartigue twenty-four years later.
August 23: Birth of Dani, Jacques Lartigue and Madeleine Messager's first child.
Jacques Lartigue dedicates more and more time to painting: bouquets, gardens, and portraits.

1922. Jacques Lartigue's paintings are exhibited for the first time, at the Galerie Georges Petit in Paris. He discovers Monet, who is exhibited in the same gallery at the same time. He later shows some of his paintings at the Salon des Sports, the Salon d'Automne, and the Salon de la Société Nationale des Beaux-Arts. This is the beginning of his career as a painter.
He meets Van Dongen, Maurice Chevalier, Abel Gance, Sacha Guitry, and Yvonne Printemps.

1923. January 1: Jacques takes his first photographs lit with magnesium flash.
August: The Château de Rouzat is sold.
Jacques Lartigue exhibits at the 16th Salon de l'Ecole Française at the Grand Palais, then at the Salon d'Hiver and at the Galerie Bernheim Jeune.
November 5: He is hired for a desk job at Paramount.
November 9: He resigns.

1924. Birth of his second child, Véronique. Yvonne Printemps is the godmother, and Sacha Guitry the godfather. Véronique will live only a few months.

1925. Jacques Lartigue shows at the Salon des Indépendants at the Grand Palais.

1929. Death of André Messager. Exhibitions at the Salon de l'Ecole Française and the Salon des Indépendants at the Grand Palais.

1930. Jacques Lartigue meets Renée Perle. He exhibits again at the Galerie Georges Petit and at the Salon d'Automne.

1931. Jacques Lartigue and Madeleine Messager's divorce is finalized.

1932. The director Granovsky hires Jacques Lartigue as assistant director on a film titled *Les Aventures du Roi Pausole*.

1933. Over the course of the year, Jacques Lartigue will participate in seven painting shows, mostly in Paris, but in Cannes as well.

1934. He marries Marcelle Paolucci, whom he nicknames Coco.

1935. Like Van Dongen and Picabia, Jacques Lartigue designs sets for gala events at the casinos in Cannes, La Baule, and Lausanne.
At the Galerie Jouvène in Marseilles, he exhibits portraits of Van Dongen, Sacha Guitry, Marlene Dietrich, Georges Carpentier, and Joan Crawford, which are a great success.

1939. Opening of Jacques Lartigue's solo exhibition in the large rooms of the Galerie Charpentier in Paris.
September 3: France goes to war against Germany.

1942. Jacques Lartigue meets Florette Orméa in Monte-Carlo.
November: The Germans take unoccupied France.

1943. Jacques and Florette witness the arrest of Tristan Bernard and his family during a raid on the Hôtel Windsor in Cannes. Florette rejoins Jacques in Paris. They live at 50 rue Desbordes-Valmore.

1944. Paris is liberated. Jacques Lartigue takes dozens of photographs.
August 25: He learns of Sacha Guitry's arrest.

1945. August 28: Jacques Lartigue marries Florette Orméa at the city hall of the 16th arrondissement in Paris. They divide their time between 4 rue Dufrénoy in Paris and Piscop in the Val-d'Oise.

1951. Jacques Lartigue, who has continued painting and selling his work, gets back in touch with the galleries he knows and exhibits in Paris again.

1954. Creation of the Gens d'Images association; Jacques Lartigue is the vice president.
Albert Plécy publishes photographs by Jacques Lartigue in the first issues of *Point de vue* and *Images du monde*.

1955. His photographs of Pablo Picasso and Jean Cocteau, taken at Vallauris, are published worldwide. Gens d'Images organizes a photography exhibition that brings together works by Brassaï, Doisneau, Man Ray, and Jacques Lartigue.

1957. Jacques and Florette Lartigue go to Havana for a painting exhibition at the Centro de Arte Cubano; Fidel Castro has just begun his guerrilla warfare in the Sierra Maestra; Jacques Lartigue is obliged to leave his paintings behind and continue his trip to Mexico and New Orleans.

1960. A period at the Villa Medici, whose director, Jacques Ibert, is Jacques Lartigue's cousin.
Purchase and decoration of the house at Opio, near Grasse.

1962. Trip to the West Coast of the United States. Jacques Lartigue passes through New York. Through Charles Rado, of the Rapho photographic agency, he meets John Szarkowski, director of the department of photography of the Museum of Modern Art, New York, who discovers his photographs from the beginning of the century.

1963. Exhibition at the Museum of Modern Art, New York: *The Photographs of Jacques Henri Lartigue*.
November 22: Assassination of President John F. Kennedy in Dallas. A ten-page article on Jacques Lartigue appears in the same issue of *Life* that reports the death of the president of the United States.

1964. Exhibition of paintings at the Knoedler Gallery in New York.

1966. On another trip to New York he becomes friendly with the photographers Hiro and Avedon. The international publication of Jacques's first book of photographs, his *Family Album*, causes his work to be known worldwide.
Exhibition as part of the Photokina in Cologne.

1968. Richard Avedon and Bea Feitler select photographs by Jacques Henri Lartigue for the book *Diary of a Century*.

1970. *Diary of a Century* is published. The French edition will appear in 1973 under the title *Instants de ma vie*.

1971. At an exhibition of his photographs at the Photographers' Gallery in London, Jacques Lartigue meets David Hockney and Cecil Beaton. The latter's designs for the costumes for *My Fair Lady* derive from Jacques Lartigue's 1911 photograph *Carriage Day at the Races at Auteuil*.

1974. Jacques Lartigue, on the steps of the Palais de l'Elysée, takes the official photograph to celebrate the seven-year term of President Valéry Giscard d'Estaing.

1975. The exhibition *Lartigue 8 x 80* at the Musée des Arts Décoratifs in Paris represents the first French retrospective of his work.
Exhibition at the Optica Gallery in Montreal.

1976. Exhibition at the Seibu Art Museum in Tokyo.

1979. Jacques Lartigue signs the deed of gift in favor of the French state of the entirety of his work (negatives and original albums).

1980. An exhibition to celebrate Jacques Henri Lartigue's gift to the state is organized by the Association des Amis de Jacques Henri Lartigue as part of the Year of Patrimony; it is held in the Galleries Nationales du Grand Palais in Paris and is titled *Bonjour Monsieur Lartigue*. 35,000 visitors come to see it in a single month and it later travels throughout the world.

1981. Opening of a permanent exhibition gallery in the Grand Palais des Champs-Elysées, with a new exhibition, *Vingt années de découverte à travers l'oeuvre de Jacques Henri Lartigue* [Twenty years of discovery through the work of Jacques Henri Lartigue].

1982. On the occasion of the opening of a new exhibition, the Association des Amis de Jacques Henri Lartigue celebrates the photographer and the eightieth anniversary of the first photograph that he took in 1902.

1984. February 29: Opening of the exhibition *Pages d'albums* at the Grand Palais in Paris.
The exhibition *London* is held at the Olympus Gallery in London.
Le passé composé. Les 6 x 13 de Jacques Henri Lartigue is presented at the Musée Réattu in Arles, during the Rencontres Internationales de la Photographie (International Photography Meeting).

1986. *Le troisième oeil de Jacques Henri Lartigue*, an exhibition of Jacques Lartigue's stereoscopic views, opens at the Grand Palais.
September 12: Jacques Lartigue dies in Nice.

Monographs

The Photographs of Jacques Henri Lartigue.
Catalogue for the exhibition at the Museum of Modern Art, New York. Introduction by John Szarkowski. 1963.

Boyhood Photos of Jacques Henri Lartigue: The Family Album of a Gilded Age.
Edited by Jean Fondin. Guichard Time Life Books, New York, 1966.

Diary of a Century.
Conceived and edited by Richard Avedon. Viking Press, New York, 1970, and Weidenfeld and Nicholson, London, 1971.

Portfolio Jacques Henri Lartigue.
Ten original signed photographs by Jacques Henri Lartigue. A limited print run of 50 copies. Introduction by Anaïs Nin. Witkin-Berley Ltd., New York, 1972.

Das Fest Grossen Rüpüskul.
Text by Elisabeth Borchers; photographs by Jacques Henri Lartigue. Insel Verlag, Frankfurt am Main, 1973.

Jacques Henri Lartigue et les femmes.
Photographs and commentary by Jacques Henri Lartigue. Studio Vista, London, 1974, and Dutton and Co., New York, 1974.

Jacques Henri Lartigue et les autos.
Photographs and commentary by Jacques Henri Lartigue. Editions du Chêne, Paris, 1974.

Mémoires sans mémoire.
Excerpts from the journal of Jacques Henri Lartigue. Editions Robert Laffont, Paris, 1975.

Lartigue 8 x 80.
Catalogue of the exhibition held at the Musée des Arts Décoratifs in Paris. Delpire éditeur, Paris, 1975.

Histoire de la photographie 2.
Jacques Henri Lartigue. Aperture Inc., New York, 1976.

Mon livre de photographie.
Editions du Chat Perché. Flammarion, Paris, 1977.

Portfolio Jacques Henri Lartigue 1903–1916.
Signed on the title page. 7,500 copies published. 10 photographs. Time Life, New York, 1978.

Les femmes aux cigarettes.
96 photographs and preface by Jacques Henri Lartigue. Conceived and produced by Sheldon Cotler Inc. Editions/The Viking Press, New York, 1980.

Les autochromes de Jacques Henri Lartigue 1912–1927.
Editions Herscher, Paris, 1980.

Bonjour Monsieur Lartigue.
Catalogue for the exhibition curated by the Association des Amis de Jacques Henri Lartigue, Paris, 1980.

Jacques Henri Lartigue.
By Henri Chapier. Collection Les Grands Photographes. Editions Belfond, Paris, 1981.

L'Emerveillé écrit à mesure 1923–1931.
Extracts from Jacques Henri Lartigue's journal. Editions Stock, Paris, 1981.

Jacques Henri Lartigue.
Text by Jacques Damade. Collection Photo-poche no. 3. Centre National de la Photographie, Paris, 1983.

Lartigue: Photographs 1970–1982.
J.M. Dent & Sons, Ltd., London, 1983.

Jacques Henri Lartigue: les femmes.
Preface by Ainslie (in French, English, German, and Italian). Catalogue for the exhibition *Femmes de mes autrefois et de maintenant*. Olympus, London, 1984.

Le passé composé. Les 6 x 13 de Jacques Henri Lartigue.
Exhibition catalogue. Text by Michel Frizot. Collection Photo Copies, Centre National de la Photographie/Association des Amis de Jacques Henri Lartigue, Paris, 1984.

L'oeil de l'oiseleur.
By Jacqueline Kellen. Editions Desclée De Brouwer, Paris, 1985.

L'oeil de la mémoire 1932–1985.
Excerpts from the journal of Jacques Henri Lartigue from 1932 to 1985. Editions Carrère-Lafon, Paris, 1986.

Jacques Henri Lartigue Albums.
Catalogue of the exhibitions *Vingt années de découverte à travers l'oeuvre de Jacques Henri Lartigue* and *Pages d'albums* presented at the Musée de l'Elysée, Lausanne, and the Helmhaus Museum, Zürich. Editions Benteli, Bern, 1986.

Jacques Henri Lartigue.
Catalogue of the exhibition *Le passé composé. Les 6 x 13 de Jacques Henri Lartigue.* Pacific Press Service, Tokyo, 1986.

Jacques Henri Lartigue.
Catalogue of the exhibition *Le bonheur du jour, 1902–1936.* Texts by Pier Luigi Pizzi, Carlo Bertelli, and Pier Luigi Ghirri. Edizioni Essegi/Teatro Municipale Valli in Reggio Emilia, 1987.

Le troisième oeil de Jacques Henri Lartigue.
Exhibition catalogue. Stereoscopic viewer. Edition Association des Amis de Jacques Henri Lartigue, Paris, 1988.

Les envols de Jacques Henri Lartigue et les débuts de l'aviation.
Exhibition catalogue. Texts by Pierre Borhan and Martine d'Astier. Editions Philippe Sers/Association des Amis de Jacques Henri Lartigue, Paris, 1989.

Rivages.
Exhibition catalogue. Text by Michel Braudeau. Editions Contrejour/Association des Amis de Jacques Henri Lartigue, Paris, 1990.

La traversée du siècle.
Text by Florette Lartigue. Editions Bordas, Paris, 1990.

Jacques Henri Lartigue: Le choix du bonheur.
By Jacques Henri Lartigue. Texts by Richard Avedon, Shelley Rice, and John Szarkowski. Collection Donation no. 6. Editions la Manufacture/Association des Amis de Jacques Henri Lartigue, Paris, 1992.

Jacques Henri Lartigue. Souvenirs de mon bonheur.
Catalogue of the exhibition held at the Galleria Art Hall, Seoul, 1994.

Jacques Henri Lartigue—Boy with a Camera.
Macmillan Publishing Co., New York, 1994.

Le Regard d'Enfant.
Le Regard d'Amour.
Le Regard du Temps.
A three-volume work. New Art Seibu, Tokyo, 1994/1995.

Jacques Henri Lartigue—La rétrospective d'un amateur génial.
Asahi Shimbun, Tokyo, 1995.

La Côte d'Azur de Jacques Henri Lartigue. Lartigue's Riviera.
Text by Mary Blume. Editions Flammarion, Paris, 1997.

Exhibitions held before Jacques Henri Lartigue gave his entire work to the French state

1955. Galerie d'Orsay, Paris. First show of the photographs of Jacques Henri Lartigue.

1963. *The Photographs of Jacques Henri Lartigue.* First solo exhibition of his work at the Museum of Modern Art, New York.

1975. *Lartigue 8 x 80.* Exhibition held at the Musée des Arts Décoratifs, Paris. First major retrospective of Jacques Henri Lartigue's photography in France.

Exhibitions curated and held by the Association des Amis de Jacques Henri Lartigue

1980. *Bonjour Monsieur Lartigue.* 155 photographs. Exhibition to celebrate Lartigue's gift to the state, in the Galleries Nationales du Grand Palais in Paris. Toured to:
- Fondation Nationale de la Photographie, Lyons, 1981.
- Musée de Sidi Bou Saïd, Tunisia, 1982.
- Galerie Hippolyte, Helsinki, 1983.
- Palais de l'Europe, Menton, 1984.
- Centre Culturel Municipal de Fréjus, 1984.
- Palais des Congrès de Nice, 1984–85.
- Mese della Fotografia, Turin, 1985.
- Franshals Museum de Hallen, Haarlem, 1985.
- Mairie de Cassis *Villégiatures des écrivains de la côte,* 1988.
- Photography Month, Athens, 1989.
- Centre de Développement Culturel, Aurillac, 1990–91.
- Rencontres de la Photographie, Coimbra, 1991.
- Hasselblad Center, Göteborg, 1992.
- Institut Français de Prague, 1994.
- Institut Français de Bratislava, 1994.
- Délégation Générale de l'Alliance Française, Brno, 1994.
- Musée du Château, Lunéville, 1995.

Catalogue

1981. *Vingt années de découverte à travers l'oeuvre de Jacques Henri Lartigue.* 89 photographs. Opening of a permanent exhibition gallery in the Grand Palais des Champs-Elysées, Paris. Toured to:
- Galleria di Piazza Navona, Rome, 1984.
- Swiss Photography Foundation, Helmhaus Museum, Zürich; Musée de l'Elysée, Lausanne, 1986.

- Centre Culturel de Brive, 1987.
- Centre Culturel Français de Berlin Est, 1988.
- Kunsthalle, Rostock, 1988.
- Galerie Marktschlösschen de Halle, 1988.
- Staatliches Lindenau-Museum, Attenburg, 1989.
- Dresden Cultural Institute, 1989.
- Kunstforeningen, Copenhagen, 1989.
- Bonn, Tübingen, Karlsruhe, Berlin, Hanover, Hamburg, Mainz, Heidelberg, Stuttgart, Saarbrücken, 1990–91.
- L'Ermitage, Rueil-Malmaison, 1994.
- Lavoir Vasserot, Saint-Tropez, 1995.
- A.C.B., Scène Nationale de Bar-le-Duc, 1996.
- Musée des Beaux-Arts, Aurillac, 1996.
- Ecole Robert Doisneau, Issy-les-Moulineaux, 1997.

Catalogue.

Sacha Guitry et Yvonne Printemps, paysages, tennis. Temporary exhibitions held at the Grand Palais, Paris.

1982. *Bonjour Monsieur Lartigue.* 125 photographs. Exhibition held at the International Center of Photography, New York. Toured to:
- Flint, Grand Rapids, Santa Barbara, Memphis, Middletown, 1983.
- Washington, D.C., Oklahoma City, Kansas City, Rockford, Claremont, 1984.
- Providence, Palm Beach, Houston, 1985.
- Printemps Ginza Department Store, Tokyo, Osaka, 1986.

Catalogue.

1983. *Femmes de mes autrefois et de maintenant.* 88 photographs. Exhibition held at the Grand Palais des Champs-Elysées, Paris. Toured to:
- Olympus Gallery, London, 1985.
- Galerie Olympus, Hamburg, 1985.
- Museu da Imagen e do Som de São Paulo, 1988.
- French Institute of Edinburgh, Manchester, Liverpool, Oldham, 1990.
- Kunstforeningen, Copenhagen, 1992.

Catalogue.

1984. *Pages d'album.* 59 photographs. Exhibition held at the Grand Palais des Champs-Elysées, Paris. Toured to:
- Swiss Photography Foundation, Helmhaus Museum, Zürich; Musée de l'Elysée, Lausanne, 1986.
- Kunstforeningen, Copenhagen, 1989.

Integrated into the exhibition *La rétrospective d'un amateur génial.*
Catalogue.

Le passé composé.
Les 6 x 13 de Jacques Henri Lartigue. 57 photographs. Exhibition held at the Musée Réattu, Arles, and the Grand Palais des Champs-Elysées, Paris, 1985. Toured to:
- Museum of Modern Art, New York, 1986.
- Art Institute of Chicago, 1986.
- North Carolina Museum of Art, Raleigh, 1988.
- San Diego Museum of Photographic Arts, 1988.
- John and Mable Ringling Museum of Art, Sarasota, Florida, 1988.
- Musée des Beaux-Arts de Montréal, 1988.
- Minneapolis Institute of Art, 1989.
- Virginia Museum of Fine Arts, Richmond, 1989.
- Crocker Art Museum, Sacramento, 1990.
- The Art Museum of South Texas, Corpus Christi, 1990.
- Konika Plaza, Tokyo; Keihan, Osaka, 1991.
- French Cultural Institute, Rome, 1992.
- Centre Culturel Français, Algiers, Tlemcen, Sidi Bel Abbes, 1993.
- Photography Month, Lisbon, 1993.
- The Royal Photographic Society, Bath, 1995.
- Musée du Château, Lunéville, 1995.
- Centro de Fotografia, Almeria, 1995.
- City of Granada, 1996.

Catalogue.

London. 35 photographs. Exhibition held at the Olympus Gallery, London.

1986. *Le troisième oeil de Jacques Henri Lartigue.* 54 photographs. Photographs in relief. Exhibition held at the Grand Palais des Champs-Elysées. Toured to:
- Tokyo, Osaka, Kyoto, Kukoka, Nagoya, 1988.
- Château de la Roche-Jagu et Saint-Brieuc, 1990.

Catalogue.

1987. *Le bonheur du jour 1902–1936.* 109 photographs. Exhibition held at the Teatro Municipale Valli in Reggio Emilia, on the occasion of the performance of the opera *The Italian Straw Hat.* Integrated in part into the exhibition *La rétrospective d'un amateur génial.*
Catalogue.

1988. *Moi et les autres.* 122 photographs. Exhibition held at the Grand Palais des Champs-Elysées, Paris. Toured to:
- Théâtre de l'Agora à Evry, 1991.
- Palais Carnoles, Menton, 1996.

1989. *Les envols de Jacques Henri Lartigue.*
84 photographs. Exhibition held at the Grand
Palais des Champs-Elysées, Paris.
Toured to:
  · Lowe Art Museum, Miami, 1993.
  · Huntsville Museum of Art, Alabama, 1993.
  · Southeast Museum of Photography, Daytona
    Beach, 1994.
  · Paine Art Center and Arboretum, Oshkosh,
    Wisconsin, 1994.
  · National Museum of Aviation, Ottawa,
    1994.
  · Cultural Services of the French Embassy,
    New York, 1995.
  · San Francisco International Airport, 1995.
  · Fresno Metropolitan Museum, 1995.
  · Air and Space Museum, Smithsonian
    Institution, Washington, D.C., 1995–96.
Catalogue.

1990. *Rivages.*
106 photographs. Exhibition held at the Grand Palais
des Champs-Elysées, Paris.
Toured to:
  · Musée de la Mer, Ile Ste Marguerite, Cannes,
    1992.
  · Théâtre de la Passerelle, Gap, 1992.
  · Centre Culturel de la Mairie de Royan, 1993.
  · Médiathèque Municipale, Issy-les-Moulineaux,
    1994.
  · Galerie "Le Lieu," Lorient, 1995.
  · Encontros da Imagem, Braga, 1995.
  · Espace Malraux, Chambéry, Savoie, 1996
  · Galerie du Centre Photographique de Normandie,
    Rouen, 1998.
Catalogue.

Volare.
50 photographs. Exhibition held at the Eralov gallery
in Rome.

1991. *Jacques Henri Lartigue à l'école du jeu.*
110 photographs. Exhibition held at the Grand Palais
des Champs-Elysées, Paris.
Toured to:
  · Nederlands Foto Instituut, Rotterdam, 1994–95.

Jacques Henri Lartigue.
62 photographs.
Toured to:
  · Tarazona, Valencia, Logrono, Pamplona,
    Gijon, Bilbao, Huesca, 1991–92.
  · French Cultural Center, Damascus, Aleppo,
    1992.

  · Saana, Yemen, Kuwait, Cairo, 1992–93.
  · CNDP in Montmorillon, CNDP in Poitiers, 1994.
  · Photo-Club of Isle-Adam, 1994.
  · Royal Photographic Society, Bath, 1995.
  · Hôtel de Ville, Le Pecq, 1995.
  · Espace Walberg, Seillans, 1995.
  · SA Nostra, Palma de Mallorca, 1996.
  · Médiacentre Fribourgeois, Fribourg, 1997.
  · Fotonoviembre 97, Santa-Cruz-de-Tenerife,
    Canary Islands, 1997.

1993. *En route Monsieur Lartigue.*
96 photographs. Exhibition held at the Grand Palais
des Champs-Elysées, Paris.
Toured to:
  · Hôtel de Sully, Paris, 1994.
  · Maison des Congrès, Clermont-Ferrand,
    1995.

1994. *Souvenirs de mon bonheur.*
81 photographs.
Toured to:
  · Galleria Art Hall, Seoul, 1994.
  · French Cultural Center of Pusan, 1994.
Catalogue.

Lartigue Centenary.
Exhibition of prints in the collection. The
Photographers' Gallery, London, 1994.

Lartigue a cent ans.
125 photographs. Exhibition held at the Rencontres
Internationales de la Photographie d'Arles and at the
Espace Electra, Paris.
Toured to:
  · Art Gallery of New South Wales, Sydney,
    1995–96.
  · Galleria Gottardo, Lugano, 1996.
  · Casino de Cavalaire-sur-Mer, 1997.
  · Galerie Française, Piazza Navona, Rome,
    1998.

1995. *Rétrospective d'un amateur génial.*
200 photographs. Exhibition held at the Bunkamura
Museum of Art, Shibuya, Tokyo, 1995.
Toured to:
  · Daimura Museum, Umeda, Osaka, 1996.
  · Hiroshima Museum of Art, 1996.
  · Umeå, 1998.
Catalogue.

1997. *La Côte d'Azur de Jacques Henri Lartigue.*
200 photographs. Exhibition at the Hôtel de Sully,
Paris, June 20–September 14, 1997.

Toured to:
  · Galerie Mossa, Nice, 1997.
  · Fotografie Forum, Frankfurt, 1998.
  · Fotografisk Center, Copenhagen, 1998.
Book in French and English, Editions Flammarion,
Paris, 1997.

Filmography

1966. *Le magicien.*
Directed by Claude Fayard. A Coty Production.

1970. *La famille Lartigue.*
Directed by Robert Hugues. Produced by O.R.T.F. for
the *Panorama* series.

1971/1972. *Jacques Henri Lartigue.*
Directed by Claude Gallot. Produced by O.R.T.F. for
the *Variances* series, no. 19.

1974. *Jacques Henri Lartigue.*
Directed by Claude Ventura. Produced by O.R.T.F. for
the *Italiques* series.

1980. *Jacques Henri Lartigue, un photographe.*
"Magazine Aujourd'hui en France," no. 24. Directed
by Fernand Moscovitz. Produced by the French
Ministry of Foreign Affairs.

1980. *Jacques Henri Lartigue peintre et photographe.*
Directed by François Reichenbach. Produced by A2,
four episodes, 30mm.

1982. *Jacques Henri Lartigue—The Great Master
of Photographers.*
Directed by Peter Adam. Produced by the Music
and Arts Department of the B.B.C.

1984. *Jacques Henri Lartigue—La Belle Epoque.*
Directed by ABC/Metropolitan Museum of Art,
New York.

1985. *Diary of a Century.*
Directed by Carl-Gustav Nykvist. Produced
by Heinrik von Sydow and Lucifer Films AB, in
cooperation with the Swedish Film Institute
and Swedish Television.

I am happy that this book exists. Jacques and I had been hoping that it would for a long time. And it is right that it should be prepared by Robert Delpire, since he was the first editor to recognize the importance of Lartigue's work. I thank him for the care that he brought to the conception and production of this publication.

I would also like to thank Albert Plécy for his very early interest in Jacques's photographs, as well as Charles Rado and John Szarkowski, who introduced them to the American public.

Finally, I could not forget the vigilant and efficient attention that Martine d'Astier de la Vigerie and the Association des Amis de Jacques Henri Lartigue brought to the introduction and dissemination of his work.

Florette Lartigue

Association des Amis de Jacques Henri Lartigue
19, rue Réaumur 75003 Paris.
Telephone 33 1 42 74 30 60/Fax 33 1 42 74 30 80

This volume was designed and produced by Robert Delpire with the collaboration of Robert Sadoux et d'Idéodis Création.
It was printed on July 30, 1998 (using prints made by Yvon le Marlec) by Jean Genoud SA, Entreprise D'Arts Graphiques, in Lausanne.